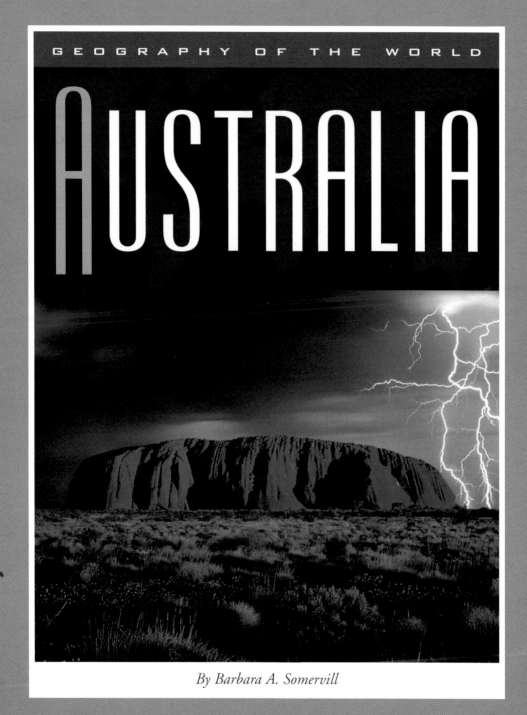

GEOGRAPHY OF THE WORLD

AUSTRALIA

By Barbara A. Somervill

THE CHILD'S WORLD®
CHANHASSEN, MINNESOTA

The Child's World

Published in the United States of America by The Child's World®
P.O. Box 326, Chanhassen, MN 55317-0326
800-599-READ
www.childsworld.com

Photo Credits: Cover: Mark Laricchia/Corbis; Animals Animals/Earth Scenes: 7 (Bates
Littlehales), 11 (Michael Fogden), 16 (Fritz Prenzel), 17 (Adrienne Gibson), 17
(Mickey Gibson); Corbis: 9, 19 (Paul A. Sounders), 14, 27 (Australian Picture
Library), 21 (Catherine Karnow), 22 (Penny Tweedie); Picture Desk: 25 (Art Archive);
Virtual Australia: 15.

The Child's World®: Mary Berendes, Publishing Director
Editorial Directions, Inc.: E. Russell Primm, Editorial Director; Pam Rosenberg, Line
Editor; Katie Marsico, Assistant Editor; Olivia Nellums, Editorial Assistant; Susan
Hindman, Copy Editor; Elizabeth K. Martin, Proofreader; Ann Grau Duvall, Peter
Garnham, Carol Yehling, Fact Checkers; Dr. Charles Maynara, Professor of Geography,
Radford University, Radford, Virginia, Subject Consultant; Tim Griffin/IndexServ,
Indexer; Cian Loughlin O'Day, Photo Researcher; Elizabeth K. Martin, Photo Selector;
XNR Productions, Inc., Cartographer

Library of Congress Cataloging-in-Publication Data
Somervill, Barbara A.
  Australia / by Barbara Somervill.
     p. cm. — (Geography of the world series)
Summary: Introduces the geography, topography, and climate of the continent
of Australia. Includes bibliographical references and index.
  ISBN 1-59296-063-4 (library bound : alk. paper)
 1. Australia—Juvenile literature. 2. Australia—Geography—Juvenile literature.
[1. Australia—Geography.] I. Title. II. Series.
  DU96.S66 2004
  919.4—dc21   2003006488

TABLE OF CONTENTS

CHAPTER ONE

WHERE IS AUSTRALIA?

ustralia is found south of the **equator.** Its location gives it

the nickname the Land Down Under. The Indian Ocean borders

Australia on the north, west, and south. The Pacific Ocean lies to the

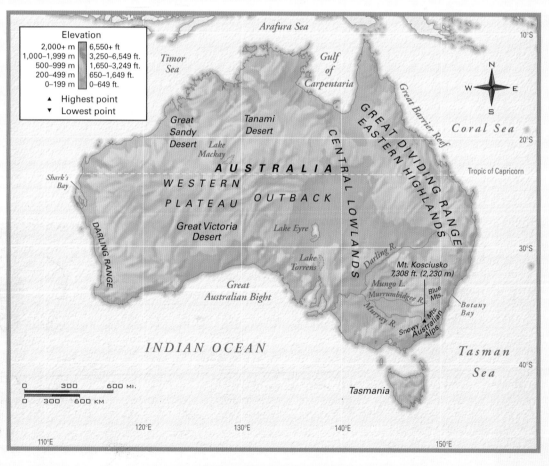

A physical map of Australia

east. The **continent** ranges from 113° to 153° east **longitude** and from 10° to 43° south **latitude.**

Some things common to North America are different in Australia. For example, the seasons are opposite. Christmas falls in the summer. July and August are rainy winter months. Moss grows on the south side of trees, not on the north side as in North America. Water flows down drains clockwise, not counter-clockwise as it does in the Northern Hemisphere.

Precipitation—mostly rain—varies from region to region.

AUSTRALIAN SEASONS			
TRADITIONAL SEASON	**MONTHS**	**ABORIGINAL SEASON**	**MONTHS**
Summer	December, January, February	Gudjewg Banggereng	December, January February, March
Fall	March, April, May	Yegge	April, May
Winter	June, July, August	Wurregeng Gurrung	June, July August, September
Spring	September, October, November	Gunumeleng	October, November

Desert areas receive less than 0.5 inch (1.25 centimeters) of rainfall each year.

Tropical rain forests in the northeast region get as much as 5 feet (1.5 meters) of rain.

For the last 10 years, Australia has suffered a **drought.** During a drought, crops die in the fields. Sheep and cattle go thirsty.

Australia is the only continent occupied by just one country. Most people live along the coast. The largest cities—Adelaide, Brisbane, Melbourne, Perth, and Sydney—are all port cities.

Farmland lies directly west of the mountainous region that runs along Australia's east cost. Australian farms are called stations. Sheep and cattle graze on grassy scrub. Wheat is also grown there.

Australia is a world leader in wool production.

Few people live in the center of Australia. This area is called the

Outback and is mostly dry or **semiarid** desert. Alice Springs is the

only Outback town of any size.

CHAPTER TWO

How Did Australia Come to Be?

Travel back in time millions of years. Back then, Australia was part of a supercontinent called Gondwanaland. Over the years, pressure from molten rock under Earth's surface pushed up against the land. Gondwanaland slowly broke apart to form South America, Africa, Antarctica, and Australia, as well as the subcontinent of India. Over time, Australia slowly drifted to the southeast. In fact, it is still moving. It edges northward about 2.25 inches (5.5 cm) each year.

Australia has been separated from other continents for millions of years. As a result, it developed plants and animals that are different from those found elsewhere. That is

DESERT DINING

Australian deserts offer plenty to eat. Try high-protein wichetty grubs, eaten raw. Ruby saltbush berries, yellow bush tomatoes, and bush onions provide vitamins. For water, suck on parakeelya leaves or squeeze water from a cyclorana frog's stomach.

Many animals, such as these wallabies, are found only in Australia.

why kangaroos, platypuses, wallabies, and hundreds of other

species are found only in Australia.

Thick tropical forests once covered the continent, but time

changed the land. By about five million years ago, most of the

land had become desert or grassland. Today, desert covers about

40 percent of the land.

Australia is the lowest, flattest, and nearly the driest of the seven

continents. Only Antarctica receives less precipitation. Australia is also the smallest continent, with only 2,967,896 square miles (7,686,850 square kilometers) total area. Three regions divide Australia—the Western **Plateau,** Central Lowlands, and Eastern Highlands.

The Western Plateau covers two-thirds of Australia. It is some of the oldest land on Earth's surface. Many of its rocks are three billion years old. Most of Australia's deserts lie on the Western Plateau. The largest deserts are the Great Victoria, Great Sandy, and Tanami. Dry lakes and riverbeds dot the region.

Low mountain ranges and grassy scrubland fill the Central Lowlands. Australia's major rivers flow through this region. The major river system is the Murray, which flows for 1,609 miles (2,589 km). Other main rivers include the Murrumbidgee and the Darling.

The limestone pillars of the Pinnacle Desert are up to 13 feet (4 meters) tall.

The Eastern Highlands contain the Australian Alps, the Blue

Mountains, and the Snowy Mountains. Australia's highest peak,

Mount Kosciusko, reaches 7,308 feet (2,228 m). The eastern coastline

is known for its beautiful sandy beaches.

CHAPTER THREE

WHAT MAKES AUSTRALIA SPECIAL?

Tourists flock to Australia to see its remarkable natural wonders.

The continent has 14 United Nations World Heritage Sites. These

places have natural or cultural importance. World Heritage Sites

include Uluru–Kata Tjuta National Park, the Great Barrier Reef, the

Tasmanian Wilderness, and the Wet Tropics of Queensland.

Uluru (Ayers Rock), the world's largest single rock, attracts tourists

for its size and deep color. As the Sun sweeps across the sky, Uluru ap-

pears to change color, from brilliant red to deep blue. Uluru and Kata

Tjuta are the remains of a once great moun-

tain range. The rocks are sacred to Australian

Aboriginals. In 1985, the government

returned Uluru to its Aboriginal owners.

SACRED ART

Aboriginal paintings tell the history of tribal cultures. Some paintings show simple hand stencils. Others tell of successful hunts or Aboriginal creation stories.

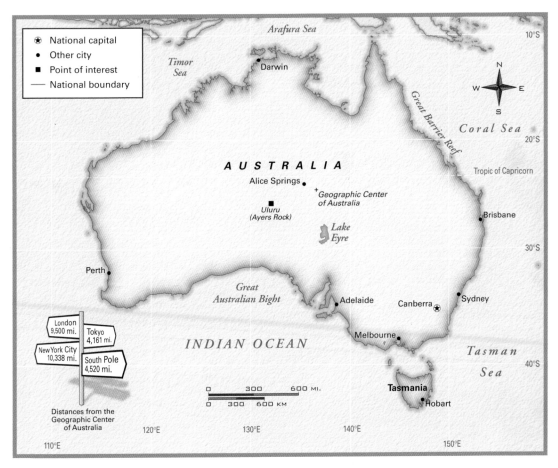

A political map of Australia

The rock's many caves are decorated with rock paintings. Some

paintings are tens of thousands of years old. Sacred areas are off-limits

to visitors.

The Great Barrier Reef is the world's largest **coral reef.** The

area consists of 3,000 connected coral reefs and about 600 islands.

The Great Barrier Reef has more than 1,500 different types of fish and covers an area of more than 180,000 square miles (289,620 sq km).

It stretches 1,240 miles (2,000 km) along the northeast coast of Australia. The reef grows and changes as old coral dies and leaves hard skeletons behind. New coral lives atop the old. About 400 different types of coral live on the reef.

Reef life is a constant game of hide-and-seek. Bright red-and-white clown fish dart in and out

of branch coral. Manta rays

and whale sharks glide through

the shallows looking for food.

An octopus slips from its home.

Shrimp and crabs, the octopus's favorite

food, scurry to hide behind sea anemones.

Eucalyptus forests are critical for the survival of many of Australia's unique animals.

The Tasmanian Wilderness covers about one-fifth of Tasmania, an

island located about 150 miles (241 km) off the southeast coast of

Australia. The area contains **temperate** rain forest, eucalyptus for-

est, grassland, and mountain **ecosystems.** Many animals here are

rare, endangered, or threatened species. Lucky visitors might spot a

Tasmanian devil, a spotted-tailed quoll, or an eastern quoll hunting in

the Tasmanian night.

Millaa Millaa Falls in the Tablelands is one of the many waterfalls that dot the landscape of northern Queensland.

The Wet Tropics of Queensland stretch along the northern coast of Australia. The area features fast-running rivers, lacy waterfalls, and dense tropical rain forests. About 390 species of rare and threatened plants thrive in the region. Many animals in the Wet Tropics are rare—even for Australia. Nowhere else can musky rat kangaroos, yellow-bellied gliders, or southern cassowaries be found.

CHAPTER FOUR

WHAT ANIMALS AND PLANTS ARE FOUND IN AUSTRALIA?

Australia is best known for its kangaroos. However, kangaroos are only one of 250 marsupial species that live on the continent. Marsupials—pouched animals—raise their young in a pocket on the mother's stomach. They are mammals. Their young drink the mothers' milk.

This gray kangaroo female feeds while her joey rides comfortably in her pouch. Top right, Aboriginals used rock art to depict animals important to them, such as kangaroos.

Kangaroo-like marsupials come in several sizes. The largest are the red or gray kangaroos. They grow to 5 feet (1.5 m) tall with 4-foot-long (1.2-m) tails. Wallabies are mid-sized—about 2 feet (60 cm) tall with a 2-foot-long (60 cm) tail. Musky rat kangaroos grow to about half the size of wallabies.

Koalas, wombats, and Tasmanian devils don't look like kangaroos, but they are still marsupials. The great glider seems more like a flying squirrel than a kangaroo. It "flies" from tree to tree in Queensland's tropical forests.

Australia's echidnas and platypuses are egg-laying mammals. Female echidnas—spiny anteaters—put their eggs into stomach pouches until they hatch. The platypus lays its eggs in a burrow. Male platypuses have spurs with poison that they inject into enemies when attacked.

Avoid Australian spiders and snakes. Australian redback and funnel web spiders are not deadly, but their bites are painful. The continent hosts several dangerous snakes—the poisonous brown, tiger, death adder, taipan, and copperhead.

Many of Australia's birds are colorful. Sulfur-crested cockatoos take flight in flocks of several hundred, painting the sky white and

An echidna is a unique anteater that uses its spiny exterior to protect itself against predators.

yellow. Pink-and-gray galahs and green-and-yellow budgerigars nibble seeds in gardens. Rainbow lorikeets snack on fruit trees in backyards.

Australia's birds range from huge, flightless emus to stunning black swans and graceful lyrebirds. Bower birds build tidy nests in the grasslands. Shy cassowaries flit through Queensland's rain forests. Across Australia, kookaburras roost in native gum trees. Their call sounds like laughter.

Australia has more than 15,500 different native plants. These include 770 varieties of wattle, or **acacia,** and 570 types of eucalyptus. Wattle blooms with bright yellow or white flowers in the spring. The eucalyptus tree's sharp-smelling oil is excellent medicine for coughs and colds.

CHAPTER FIVE

WHO LIVES IN AUSTRALIA?

A *Kadaitja,* an Aboriginal elder, gazes into the fire. He sends a mental message to other tribes on the "Mulga Wire." The tribes are camped more than 100 miles (161 km) apart. There is no wire, no phone, and no radio. Yet, six weeks later,

An Aboriginal stands in front of Uluru, or Ayers Rock as Europeans have named it. Many Aboriginals still travel on foot across the vast Australian outback.

the tribes meet for a **corroboree** in the exact same place on the exact same day. How the message arrived remains a mystery.

Australia's Aboriginals have lived for thousands of years in places that few people of European ancestry could survive. They studied the desert. It showed them how to find water in barren land. They learned to track animals over solid rock and move invisibly through dense forests.

Aboriginal children learn skills necessary for survival, such as hunting, at an early age.

As recently as 20 years ago, Aboriginals who had never seen white people still lived in Australia. They used the same tools their ancestors used a thousand years ago: a boomerang, fire sticks, spears, and stone knives. They lived as one with the land.

No one knows for sure how long Aboriginals have lived in Australia. It may be 50,000 years or even 100,000 years. When Europeans first arrived in Australia, there were about 500 Aboriginal clans. They lived as hunter-gatherers. The men hunted emus, kangaroos, and wallabies. The women gathered fruits, nuts, and berries. People also ate fungi, insects, and grubs. Honey ants provided sweet snacks.

The first European to explore Australia was Abel Tasman, a Dutch sea captain. In the 1640s, Tasman landed on an island south of the mainland. He named the island Van Diemen's Land. Today, it is called Tasmania. The first English ship to reach Australia arrived in 1688. William Dampier anchored his pirate ship in Shark's Bay on the west coast.

MUNGO PEOPLE

In 1969, a scientist found most of a skeleton near Lake Mungo in the Willandra Lakes region of New South Wales. This region now carries water only at the peak of a flood. The bones belonged to a woman who died about 26,000 years ago. Her body had been cremated (burned) and buried. Mungo Woman's bones are the oldest evidence of cremation anywhere in the world. Five years later, the bones of Mungo Man were discovered. Red ochre—a natural pigment or coloring material—was spread over his body during the burial ritual. This discovery provided scientists with evidence of the oldest known ceremonial burial in the world.

England's Captain James Cook set sail in the *Endeavour* in 1768. His mission was to find *Terra Incognita Australis,* the "unknown southern land." In 1770, the *Endeavour* sailed into a bay, now called Botany Bay. Cook claimed the continent of Australia for England. The things they found there surprised Cook and his crew. England had no animals like koalas, kangaroos, or emus. Naked Aboriginals shocked the stuffy Englishmen. Cook's ship returned to England with tales of amazing creatures—both animal and human.

England decided to use Australia as a prison colony for murderers, thieves, and debtors. English convicts worked like slaves. They earned no money for working in gold mines or on farms.

A drawing of Sydney in the early 19th century from George Barrington's History of New South Wales

The English settlers treated the Aboriginals the same way

Europeans treated Native Americans. Aboriginals did not believe in

owning land, but the English did. They took land and forced

Aboriginals into slavery. They made them wear clothing and become

Christians. Often, enslaved Aboriginals escaped by disappearing into

the Outback.

CHAPTER SIX

WHAT IS AUSTRALIA LIKE TODAY?

Australia is home to more than 19,500,000 people. The country is about the size of the continental United States, with a population about the same as New York State. Most Australians live in or near major cities. Sydney is the largest city.

THE FLYING DOCTOR SERVICE

Outback residents have no local doctors or hospitals. The Royal Flying Doctor Service provides medical care. Patients get medical advice by radio. Doctors can fly in and take seriously sick or injured patients to a hospital. There are 15 flying doctor bases, complete with aircraft, doctors, nurses, pilots, and hospitals.

Nine out of 10 people in Australia are Caucasian. The Asian population is growing quickly, however. Nearly one out of 10 people came to Australia from Asia. Aboriginals now account for less than one out of every 100 people living there.

Australia's economy is based on mining and farming. Bauxite, coal, copper, gold, and iron ore are mined there.

Farming produces grapes, wheat,

and olives. Sheep stations pro-

duce wool and meat.

Downtown Sydney

Sheep and cattle stations are like

huge Texas cattle ranches. Station life is

remote. Children who live on stations attend the "School of the Air."

This school offers classes via television and a two-way radio. Students

get their schoolbooks through the mail.

Australia is a land of great diversity. It has large cities and

remote stations, modern technology and ancient Aboriginal culture.

Residents and visitors alike enjoy its natural beauty and unusual

wildlife. Separated from the other continents for millions of years,

its unique features provide an experience like no other.

Glossary

Aboriginals (ab-uh-RIJ-uh-nuhls) Aboriginals are the native peoples of Australia who were living there long before the Europeans arrived.

acacia (uh-KAY-shuh) An acacia is a small tree or shrub with feathery leaves and white or yellow flowers. It grows in warm regions of the world.

continent (KON-tuh-nuhnt) A continent is one of the seven large landmasses on Earth.

coral reef (KOR-uhl REEF) Coral is formed when the skeletons of tiny sea creatures and other materials hardens into rock. A coral reef is a strip of coral that is close to the surface of the ocean.

corroboree (cohr-ROB-uh-ree) A corroboree is an Aboriginal meeting where the people hold sacred rites and ceremonies.

drought (DROUT) A drought is a long period during which little or no rain or other precipitation falls.

ecosystems (EE-koh-siss-tuhms) Ecosystems are communities of plants and animals interacting with their environments.

equator (i-KWAY-tur) The equator is an imaginary line that circles Earth halfway between the North and South Poles.

latitude (LAT-uh-tood) Latitude is the position of a place on the globe as it is measured in degrees north or south of the equator.

longitude (LON-juh-tood) Longitude is the position of a place on the globe as it is measured in degrees east or west of an imaginary line known as the prime meridian. The prime meridian runs through the Greenwich Observatory in London, England, and is sometimes called the Greenwich Meridian.

plateau (pla-TOH) A plateau is a raised, flat area of land.

precipitation (pri-sip-i-TAY-shuhn) Precipitation is the falling of all types of moisture from the sky, including rain, snow, sleet, and hail.

semiarid (SEM-ee A-rid) Semiarid means "half-dry" and refers to land where little rain falls.

species (SPEE-sheez) A species is a group of animals or plants that share certain characteristics.

temperate (TEM-pur-it) A climate that is temperate has temperatures that are neither very high nor very low.

An Australian Almanac

Location on the Globe:
Longitude: 113° east to 153° east
Latitude: 10° south to 43° south

Greatest distance from north to south: 1,950 miles (3,138 km)

Greatest distance from east to west: 2,475 miles (3,983 km)

Borders: Indian Ocean, Pacific Ocean

Total Area: 2,978,147 square miles (7,713,364 sq km)

Highest Point: Mount Kosciusko, 7,308 feet (2,227 m) above sea level

Lowest Point: Lake Eyre, 52 feet (16 m) below sea level

Number of Countries on the Continent: 1

Major Mountain Ranges:
Great Dividing Range

Major Deserts: Simpson, Gibson, Great Sandy, Great Victoria

Major Rivers: Murray, Murrumbidgee, and Darling

Major Lakes: Australia's natural lakes are dry most of the time. They fill only after heavy rains and can remain dry for years at a time. They include Lake Eyre, Lake Torrens, Lake Gairdner, and Lake Frome.

Major Cities:
Sydney
Melbourne
Brisbane
Adelaide
Perth
Hobart
Canberra

Languages: English, Aboriginal

Population: 19,222,000 (estimated 2000)

Religions: Christianity, Judaism, Islam

Mineral Resources: Bauxite, diamonds, lead, coal, copper, gold, iron ore, manganese, nickel, opals, silver, tin, titanium, zinc, zircon

Australia in the News

544 million to 505 million B.C.	Central Australia is covered by a shallow sea.
385 million B.C.	Massive movement of the Earth's crust in eastern Australia push the land high above sea level.
280 million B.C.	Glaciers cover much of Australia.
248 million to 145 million B.C.	Volcanos erupt in Queensland.
65 million to 3 million B.C.	Australia's low-lying coasts are flooded.
50 million B.C.	Antarctica breaks away from the landmass it shares with Australia to become a separate continent.
50,000 B.C.	Aboriginals migrate to Australia from Southeast Asia.
A.D. 1640	Dutch explorer Abel Tasman explores Tasmania.
1688	English pirate William Dampier reaches the west coast of Australia.
1770	Captain James Cook reaches Australia and claims the continent for England.
1788	The first European colonists arrive in Australia.
1850	The University of Sydney, the first university on the continent, is founded.
1851	Gold is discovered in Australia and people from all over the world arrive on the continent to seek their fortunes.
1901	The Commonwealth of Australia is founded.
1927	Canberra, the new capital city of Australia, is dedicated.
1956	Australia hosts the Olympic Games.
1980	The federal government of Australia establishes the Aboriginal Development Commission.
2000	The Olympic Games are held at Sydney, Australia.
2002 – 2003	Damaging brush fires burn outside Sydney and in the capital of Canberra.

How to Learn More about Australia

Books about Australia

Bartlett, Anne. *The Aboriginal Peoples of Australia.*
Minneapolis: Lerner Publications, 2001.

Darlington, Robert. *Australia.* Austin, Tex.: Raintree Steck-Vaughn, 2000.

Gutnik, Martin J. *Great Barrier Reef.* Austin, Tex.: Raintree Steck-Vaughn, 1994.

Hintz, Martin, and Ann Heinrichs. *Australia (Enchantment of the World).*
Danbury, Conn.: Children's Press, 1998.

Sayre, April Pulley. *Australia.* Brookfield, Conn.: Millbrook Press, 1998.

Web Sites about Australia

Visit our home page for lots of links about Australia:
http://www.childsworld.com/links.html
Note to Parents, Teachers, and Librarians: We routinely verify our Web links to make
sure they're safe, active sites—so encourage your readers to check them out!

Places to Visit or Contact

AUSTRALIAN MUSEUM
To visit Australia's first museum and learn more
about the continent and its cultures
6 College Street Sydney
NSW 2010 Australia
+612 9320 6000

EMBASSY OF AUSTRALIA
To write for more information about Australia
1601 Massachusetts Avenue, N.W.
Washington, DC 20036
800/242-2878

Index

About the Author

Barbara Somervill is the author of many books for children. She loves learning and sees every writing project as a chance to learn new information or gain a new understanding. Ms. Somervill grew up in New York State, but has also lived in Toronto, Canada; Canberra, Australia; California; and South Carolina. She currently lives with her husband in Simpsonville, South Carolina.